Cathartic Rambling

Daneasha Zackery

BookLeaf
Publishing

India | USA | UK

Made with ❤ on the BookLeaf Publishing Platform

www.bookleafpub.in

www.bookleafpub.com

Dedication

To those who encouraged me to speak when I had
resigned to a lifetime of silence.
Thank you for reminding me that my voice is indeed
mine.

Preface

Poetry was something I had avoided in my life. I had no interest in listening to people, "lie to me with flowery words". Younger me was trying so hard to be a cynic back then. Then came my high school freshman English class, and much to my dismay, a teacher who loved poetry. She said she wasn't trying to make us love the medium as much as she herself did. All she wanted us to realize was that words matter: what you say and how you say it matters. She would be proud if anything we came across made us feel something. That's all she asked, was to allow ourselves to feel if the occasion arose.

That year I fought my hardest not to be swayed. I tried to pretend that the descriptive words and metaphors that others had managed to pull out of themselves weren't inspiring me.

Obviously, that is a battle I lost. As a self proclaimed "feeler" I have always had big emotions. Sometimes I felt like they would swallow me up and consume me if I tried to keep them inside my head or heart. Poetry gave me a way to release it. Whatever the thought, feeling, or experience: I now had a way to let it exist outside of myself. These things that demanded to be acknowledged were now not a threat, but a keepsake.

They became snapshots, and tangible evidence that I was

here. No matter how many times I felt like my words or actions didn't mean anything, these poems remind me that my words, and actions, and I myself matter simply because I am here. We all matter, because we are here. No matter how long or short our existence ends up being: any being who has ever breathed or felt anything is linked by the human condition.

To create in this confounding world is a feat worthwhile. I have taken my internal monologs, gathered over the years, and compiled them into this tangible thing. A book to share with anyone who might come across it and be curious. So welcome fellow human, to my chaotic ramblings for the sake of catharsis.

Acknowledgements

To my family and friends - if you have ever encouraged me to be myself, I sincerely thank you. All the people who have ever been a force in my life, if you think I'm talking about you then I am. Love you tons.

To BookLeaf Publishing for helping me create a tangible collection of my poems. I am grateful to be able to share my words in this capacity.

A Girl

An accident. A disappointment til the end of time
the best and worst thing that you've ever seen
the world's greatest contradiction
a failing overachiever
has no faith, yet believes in everything
stressed and tranquil
relaxed while tense
an ignorant genius
a beautiful monster
spreading truthful lies
watching the purest wonders of the world with
deceiving eyes
causing shimmering tears of disastrous hope
with fragile hands she destroys everything she touches; a
devil in disguise
she wants to save the world; an angel flying high
protector and destroyer of all that she owns
heart racing; pulse low
stuck while moving at hyper speed
no heart. No head. A nothing. Dead.
Passionate brilliance radiates high
all at once. Everything. Alive.
Wanted and desired throughout the world
this is what it means to be a girl

Note to Self

Hi. I'm that person you used to know. We were never quite friends, but we acknowledged each other's existence. Now I'm that person you avoid. When I look at you, you refuse to make eye contact. In fact, you turn and look away like the sight of me makes you uneasy. You don't speak to me anymore either. In the past we had our fair share of laughs and happy memories, but now you can't spare a passing glance or a wave. I was under the impression that maybe you cared about me, but I guess I was wrong. I remember the last time you actually looked my way, the look on your face said what your lips suppressed: I sicken you. For whatever reason you have decided that I am not worth the energy it takes to stop and nod when you see a familiar face. Although it makes me sad, I am still hopeful. Hopeful that one day you will be able to face me again. Who knows, one day you may even be able to look at me and smile

-sincerely, the girl who can longer look in the mirror

Conditional

Love always seemed so conditional to me.

Like, "I love you today" or, "I love you because things went my way".

It was never, "things aren't perfect, but I love you anyway".

It was never, "love is love and that's okay".

I try to love without condition, but it never comes across that way.

When I hold you close I'm not trying to steal your warmth.

I'm merely trying to close the distance that will inevitably form between us.

I don't want to take from you. Keep every piece of yourself.

You are not an object to split and ration away. You are a whole.

A beautiful collection of pieces that don't quite fit. You shouldn't have to rip yourself apart just to fill another person's cracks.

Your mosaic is sacred, don't you know that?

Every bit of jumbled mess was placed just so that when the sun hits your outsides I see your soul glow from within.

Consider me a humble spectator. I admire you as the art

you are.

I look at the jagged edges and complex shapes and I wonder how you have yet to be marked as the eighth wonder of the world.

You are scattered here and sprawled over there, but the space you take up must feel honored to contain the shards of the most beautiful disaster that was ever created.

You are in pieces it's true, but all of those pieces are unmistakably you.

So as you pull away from my embrace remember to look for hands that don't want to take.

If greedy hands grasp at your gifts walk away.

Know that you are worth affection and admiration that wants to protect your treasures, not pillage them.

I never wanted your warmth, it is yours to keep.

Just like I never wanted this distance that you insist on giving me.

I wanted to love you without condition, but you just wanted to leave. Gathering up those pieces that I guess just weren't meant for me.

I guess my love was too snug and started to smother instead.

So from now on I'll just learn to love what used to be, instead.

My Mother's Daughter

I feel most like my mother's daughter on days where I am lonely.

Defined by the absence of all that is tangible.

I float along, somewhere between this world and the next, wondering if existing will always be so exhausting.

I think of her tears as I wipe mine, and wonder if sadness can be genetic.

Is it possible to pass depression down through chromosomes that ache with the burden of a broken heart?

Does her sadness run through my veins? Or did the tears she cried on my shoulder simply seep down into my psyche?

Was I born or bred to be the type of lonesome that can never forget what 2 a.m. feels like when the crying stops your breathing?

When every breath feels like it is chipping away at my lungs I inhale even deeper, wondering if this will be the breath that breaks me.

Breaking is all I know how to do lately.

I cannot decide if there is more or less of me these days.

My scattered bits seem to fill every empty room with a nothingness so great that even silence runs away.

There is never quiet. Never solace from sound.

When quiet comes to play my rickety heart plays me the song of unrest in the key of anxiety.
If quiet comes to play my ears ring with phantom calls.
I cannot forget the sound of my mother's tears. I cannot forget what broken looks like.
It used to be a mother wrapped in her daughter's arms.
Now it's a woman ashamed to be her mother's daughter on the days where she wishes to be anything else.

Letting Go

I've never been good at letting go. I guess that's how I
ended up with this corpse in my bed.
I wish I had gotten a ghost: they flow, there is motion,
they leave.
Non-offensive entities just trying to find a path to
freedom, and if their presence leads to discomfort you
can suspend belief and simply pretend they are not there.

But a corpse causes great offense.
They are stale, stagnant burdens even heavier than they
seem.
How can one ignore the weight and stench of a rotting
rapport?

Time unforgivingly takes the things we convince
ourselves that we cannot live without, and every time I
lose another meaningful piece of life I collect another
corpse.
Musty husks of what used to be. Morbid reminders of
what will never be again.
I take these lifeless bodies that don't mean a thing and
force feed them memories and emotions hoping to revive
what I know is gone.
These gutted cadavers will never breathe life, no matter

how many times I call them by your name and will your soul back to mine.

We were once intertwined, but now separation is the only permanence between us.
I convince myself this parting is only temporary, and tightly clutch at empty remains.
Corpses, regrets, lies: at this point I don't even know what to call them anymore.
All I know is that they are the only things still keeping this bed warm, because they are the only things I have left to hold on to.

Severance

Severance is a funny thing. Undoing the things that connected us.

The unintertwining of fingers, the unfluttering of hearts, the butterflies' wings stop flapping.

The child loses that spark in their eyes when they look up at their parents. No longer looking up at someone, only looking down on them.

What makes a bond?

Is it nature or nurture?

Did I starve us or were we simply not written in the stars?

Did you breed badly or cultivate this trauma in me? Growing like a cancer, slowly, steadily, until it is all consuming.

What makes a bond?

These ties that link us seemingly stretching to infinity.

These ties that decay just like my bruised psyche.

These ties that damage everything they are able to coil around and constrict the life out of.

Once strong, they are hanging by a thread, beyond repair.

So I cut the tie that's barely even there, but I unravel just the same.

I come undone at the thought of you. At your memories

that haunt the halls of my head like ghosts.

My pieces break a part and I finally understand that the only thing keeping me together was the delusion that you were benign. That you were something I could heal from.

But you got too deep under my skin, and penetrated parts of me I didn't know I had.

You spread through me and carved out every ounce of hope I had at survival.

The facade has been cracked, my bubble burst and I see that life without you is impossible, because life with you has already killed me.

No sparkles to be seen. My butterflies are dead. My once fluttering heart can only muster a sluggish, faint pump. Its pitiful patter now the lullaby I use to steal moments of solace in the wake of my sobering loneliness.

Fragments

What once was has been replaced by an all too resounding absence.

Be it knowledge or memory, I cannot seem to place where these intangibles belong.

Were they ever really mine if lost so easily?

Can one own what cannot be touched?

For the brain to grasp what the hands cannot seems contradictory, so why do these thoughts keep slipping through my fingers?

This vanishing act is making me uneasy.

It's like my memories are wearing masks to hide their true identity, and for some odd reason they are dead set on tricking me.

Reality is bending, switching known to forgotten, killing my confidence and leaving my assurance in a coffin.

I can't lay these worries to rest, and the anxiety paralyzes me.

For how can one trust anything when your mind fractures into infinity?

Graceless

I've got all this ringing in my ears, but no one answers
when I call. It's like I'm never alone, but always so lonely.
I've got these voices in my head who are always
whispering and calling. It's like I'm being haunted by all
those relationships that are dead.
I can't see it, but I can feel it, all this emptiness around
me. Waiting to swallow me up if I ever stop running.
The darkness scares me because I can't face myself. All
the silence and lack of distraction.
The thought of being left with nothing but the truth is a
terrifying fate, but one that I cannot seem to escape.
Some days I want it to be over, then others I don't want
it to end. Battling all these demons who disguise
themselves as kin.
No good nor evil, just grey areas of me. Patiently waiting
to see how cruel the end will be.
Time slips away but keeps me frozen all the same,
wondering if all the trying will prove to be in vain.
Uncertainty surrounding and closing in.
I guess there's nothing left to do but face these things,
because either way I'm falling without any wings.

Bankruptcy

I invested every single part of myself into you, but I guess I didn't account for depreciation. The currency of me has proven worthless to you.

The deficit left our love in debt, and you sold me out to pay your dues.

You ripped me a part and auctioned off what was left to the highest bidder.

I don't own myself anymore.

The deed to these hallowed halls of a human are still in your name.

Even still, you refuse to claim me.

I am an embarrassment: a failed investment that has tarnished your portfolio.

And much to your dismay, no matter how many times you throw me away I keep coming back.

Unlike you I cannot walk away from this. I am bound by emotion.

Your prisoner. A burden. I weigh you down with frivolous memories and begrudging guilt.

Never enough. No matter how many appraisers endorse my worth, you still argue that I am no more than fool's gold.

I beg to be valuable enough for you to acknowledge my existence, but you turn a blind eye to my spectacle.

Your heart is bankrupt, empty, and cold.

I am nothing to you, but I would still spend my last dime to see the light shine again in your eyes.

I would take bare hands to concrete and steel, rebuild you from the ground up.

I would go broke to see you standing.

Unlike you my love is not conditional, it cannot be bought nor sold.

You can ignore me as no more than junk you have accumulated.

You can starve me of your affections until I perish, and even still: with my last breath I would thank you for being the best thing I ever got to spend my time on.

For a fleeting moment you were mine and no amount of resentment could ever undermine that, to me, you are priceless.

Although I went broke trying to buy your reciprocation, I wouldn't trade our story for all the riches in this world.

True treasure cannot be quantified and no arbitrary number can express what you mean to me.

Sadly, I have nothing left. You have robbed me of everything.

So I'll give you one last thing. I'll stay behind this time.

I'll accept my place among everything else you have tossed aside.

I'll sit here, in the distance, left behind.

Who knows, maybe once you're gone I'll appreciate in value and be worth something again.

Thankful

I'm as broken as I've ever been, but I've never been more thankful.

These pieces I have divided into are distinctly me.

Although you tore me to pieces, I discovered myself in the aftermath.

I have never been more me.

I forgot myself in learning you.

I lost myself in loving you.

I found myself in losing you.

But to say where I was before you is impossible.

I knew nothing of my own hopes, dreams, or fears.

You unearthed me: with every touch, tear, and fight I was forged into my own being.

You sparked fires I never knew I possessed.

And although they eventually engulfed me I still know nothing of regret.

I do not recognize the sadness in grief.

I can't deny that I'm still mourning a love so pure and fierce that it gives me pause, but to call it a failure would be a cruel oversight.

I lost so much the day you stopped being mine, but what I have gained from this journey is so precious even the theif of time cannot erase it.

Hands on clocks go around aimlessly, just like the

thoughts in my head.

For even though I wish you were still here, I'll still be alone in this bed.

So I'll thank you for the memories, and knowing when to bow out gracefully.

You left me, it's true. All alone, without you. Guiding me to myself in a way that no one else could.

So I thank you for that, even though you don't think that I should.

At the end of the day, there's not much to say. Our love came and went, and now it's gone away.

But the mark you left on my heart will persist, for as long as it beats.

Because if I never met you, I never would have found me.

All Is Well

Is everything okay?

Eyes sting with the threat of tears.

Is everything okay?

Panic attacks steal my breath away.

Is everything okay?

Adrenaline surges through my body; is it time to fight or fly now? And what's the difference anyhow?

My exists are never graceful. My escapes leave me fractured, self-esteem in shards.

I grapple with the rigid remains of once delicate cargo. Now harsh and unforgiving.

The edges are thick enough to cut through all this tension in the air.

I've forged a weapon, a jagged piece of shrapnel from a clumsy attempt at fleeing. Maybe this is my true nature. Time to fight.

Running won't work, for how does one escape themselves?

Warrior. The concept sparks between my synapses and a smile dances across my lips.

Only for a second, but in that instance I see a chance for retribution. For offerings of fruitful possibilities.

I see the chance to stand and stay.

I have the high ground now. Isn't perspective a powerful

tool?

From this angle I no longer see an empty, abandoned husk.

From up here the sun hits my skin and illuminates all that I am, all that I ever was, and all that I could be.

At this vantage point I can see directly into my soul: I weep for who I was and all the casualties; pieces of me I left behind just trying to survive. I pay homage to who I am, because I know what it took to get here. I pray for who I will become, because heaven have mercy for a gentle soul who uses the most precious parts of themselves as a means to survive.

Whether we bargain it away like depreciated currency, or gauge it out of ourselves to use in battle, this is for the ones who manage to survive after failed attempts at fleeing.

To those who have nothing left, but will never stop.

Is it really okay not to be okay?

And if it is, how does one summarize the nuances of a not so simple, "no"?

How do I stress the extent of my exhaustion, and the soreness of this aching self?

How do I catalog my fall from grace and my alienation from everything that surrounds me?

And what's more: do you deserve to hear my harrowing tale?

Should I personify vulnerability and leave myself to be

quantified and judged?

Is everything okay?

The question pierces and provokes.

So I sigh, look you straight in the eyes, and lie: "All is well".

Imprint

Tools of torture dipped in honey: sticky, painful, sweet.
I look at you and smile, it's my way of admitting defeat.
The web of lies is camouflaged as a soft place to land, but
in the end I'm always stuck here in the palm of your
hand.
Our battles are like a dance of elegance and chaos: with
every single move we get closer to the edge, and I
wonder if this rope you've thrown can save me from this
ledge.
I know you mean it as a noose, but you might show
mercy if I beg.
The pedestal you put me on is nothing more than show,
you'll surely push me to my demise when there's no
reason left to gloat.
Once a shining spectacle for you to brag and boast: I'm
left here rotten, stained, and harsh from all the "love" you
gave.
I hate the way I love you, down to my very core,
acquiring these bruises that you'll never answer for: and
here I sit in disbelief as I try to heal myself.
Branded by the scars of you, it's my own personal hell.

Convenient

Deals, deals, deals: we got 'em. Come shop my store of regrets.
Bargain bins of self disgusts are right next to disdain.
Buy one get one apathy, but only if you're late.
Picking through my ins and outs like there's garbage on these shelves. If you don't want my inner thoughts then I'll sell them by myself.
Wading through this mess I've made: broken spirit and unsound mind.
Come and meet me at the till, I'll give you a discount, it's fine.
Banning you from parts of me when you refuse to pay, the currency is just belief, I'm pretty simple that way.
Yet you always try to steal and shoplift me away, like I'm not even worth the time of day it takes to sit and stay.
Get out and come back when you have some sense, after all at the end of the day this is still a business.
Selling all the parts of me, everything must go, I can't even remember the last time I was considered whole.
Shamefully I falter and let you in again, even though pennies is the only profit I will see.
Convincing me it's all I'm worth, you're a better salesman than me.
Here I am in pieces that I thought would be worth more,

but split a part and rationed, they're still sitting in this store.

My one and only patron, please help me save some face, this whole shop is on clearance, don't leave me here to waste.

I'll even give you coupons, so come inside post haste.

I'm willing to let you haggle, mostly out of fear.

You are un-disinvited, I'm simply delighted to have you here.

I would do most anything to exit these four walls: this air constricting barricade disguised as a shopping stall.

Free me from this burden, confined inside no more.

Sweet relief is all I feel when walking out of this door.

I've left my broken pieces, and I forgot to mourn, now I guess I'll never know what all that pain was for.

The Collector

He would always carry the strangest things.

Once I went through his pockets and pulled out a handful of misery.

There was a denim jacket filled with despair and I swear his pocket watch only showed wasted time.

His shoes were wrapped in regret from all the places he would never admit that he had been.

Although he was fun to kiss, his lips were laced in heartache, and I always wondered why that's what he picked to lubricate his lies.

His heartbeat was incomplete and I think he was out looking for whatever miscellaneous item could complete the complex sput and putter of rusted cogs that got doused in his own tears, and then dissolved under the weight of all his disappointments.

So these were his spare parts. Any old thing would do.

One night while out scavenging he found me, maybe the most peculiar item of all, but I seemed to fit.

That never stopped him from carrying his collection of oddities though.

He just couldn't seem to put down anything he had picked up.

Perhaps that's what really broke my heart: at the end he refused to carry me.

To take me with him, wherever that may be.
So as I pick up pieces of self doubt and riffle through
piles of denial, I think of my collector man and how
everything he ever found was worth keeping.
Except for me that is.

Questions

How do you feel about poetry?
And does looking up at the stars make you feel more or
less alone in this world?
Do you think you can miss people you haven't even met
yet?
Do we ever really grow up, or do we just grow around
who we used to be?
How do you feel about love?
And once you've been in it can you truly ever be out?
Can you teach your heart to stop yearning for what once
was?
How do you feel about faith, and trust, and pixie dust?
Tell me how do you feel about magic?
Is it just for children and fools, or can the rest of us
partake in the nonsensical too?
How do you feel about fear?
And why do the things I wish for with all my heart scare
me the most?
How do you feel about time? Is there enough of it for me
to find you when I haven't even finished finding myself
yet?
How do you feel loved, because God knows I want to do
right by you.
I want to know what you think, and why you feel the

way that you do about everything, even if it seems insignificant and ridiculous to you.

I know I don't know you, and you don't know me, but in time I think we'll make our way to each other eventually. This is for you, wherever you are.

When we finally cross paths I'll ask you a favor, no matter how strange it may seem: can I read you something I wrote for you back when you were nothing but a dream?

Failing To Breathe

Loving you is more natural than breathing to me.
I always feel so awkward when I try to fill my lungs: like
there is always too much, or not enough air.
I often wonder why I can't seem to get it just right,
especially when it's a skill I need to live.
It's the most basic form of existing.
People often say, "just breathe".
Just. As if it's supposed to be simple.
As if I'm the only person alive who is fighting for every
breath.
No matter how simple they try to make it seem,
breathing never gets any easier.
It never feels natural.
I've never felt particularly attached to any building, city,
or state; so the concept of home always felt foreign to
me.
I never felt like there was anywhere I could ever belong
or miss being, until I found myself in your arms.
Home is your eyes looking at me like you're telling me
everything you wouldn't dare say out loud, and knowing
that I hear every word that's unspoken.
Home is your smile reminding me that even though
nothing is perfect there is still beauty all around us.
Home is the comfort I feel every single time I remember

that you and I share a planet, and a sky, and a love.
Home is the thought of you existing at the same time
that I'm existing, and the gratitude that comes with that
fact.
Home is knowing no matter how things end, nothing can
erase the marks you left by allowing me to exist next to
you.
Home is you.
So when I'm struggling to fill my lungs, when I cannot
escape the fact that I will never master the art of human
existence, I remember how I have mastered the art of
loving you.
Loving you is the best thing I've ever done.
It's the only thing that has ever come naturally to me.
I think I've managed to learn two things during this
lifetime:

    1. I'll never be any good at breathing
    2. I don't know how to not love you

Tattoos

I got a dream catcher to stop the nightmares that had
been plaguing me for years.
I got a wolf to denote my strength, both in solitude and
as a member of community.
I've got snowflakes to honor my mother, myself, and our
complicated bond.
I've got my favorite laboratory glassware housing a
jellyfish as a commentary on being a black chemist in
academia.
All of these images litter my skin, as a tribute and
reminder of where I have been.
Aesthetic art that tells bewildering tales of blunders and
triumph, resilience and fails.
An abstract piece to give shape to the plight of a mental
health journey I've been on for life.
A geometric band wraps my arm in a pattern so I never
forget: I am neither too much nor not enough, just
because I am odd.
The shapes are all odd sided, kind of like me, and still as
capable as any shape at functionality.
Each a whole, fulfilling image, no need to be revised. So
when I look at myself I remember all the ways in which I
have been alive.

Ink Stain

I'm the creative type, I'll make something out of nothing
every chance that I get.
I'm the emotional type, I've got feelings so complex that
they swell and break a part into infinity.
I'm the inquisitive type, asking questions that can only
lead to confusion.
I'm the simple type, what you see is what you get; except
for when it's not, and I promise you it's not.
No need to worry, I've never broken a promise that
didn't mean anything and my words tend to equate to
nothing.
I'm the type that lies when it matters, because my truth
is the only thing that this world has left me with.
So I twist it and shift it into something unrecognizable. I
make it nonsensical and undecipherable.
I hide it in poems and subliminal messages: like a frown
or a tear drop. Hoping it survives what other parts of me
did not.
I'm the type that does, and does it so well that I always
mess something up.
I'm a talker and a thinker, though you can't always tell:
with a smile from heaven and a mind going through hell.
Just do me a favor and pretend I was quiet. If they found
out I've been divulging, my nightmares would riot.

You see the smile hides the darkness that never seems to ebb, and these poems are a playground for when I'm not doing so well.

I play with words and concepts that dance across my mind, giving them a way out of this cage that confines. The words are all I have, that's the truth I've been trying to hide. But now that it's said, I'm all out of rhymes. Pages and paper, words soaked in ink, passages chronicling the life of me.

At my wits end and I don't know who to tell, that's why my notebook knows me so well.